Fostering a Sense of Belonging in the Classroom

Culture, Community, Communication

Rebecca J. Speelman, Ed.D.

Fostering a Sense of Belonging in the Classroom: Culture, Community, Communication.

Copyright © 2020 by Rebecca J. Speelman

ISBN: 978-1-7345703-2-8

www.whybalancematters.com

dr.rebecca.speelman@gmail.com
ATCE: All Things Considered Education

Proudly Printed in USA

This book is dedicated to our teachers and our classroom communities! It is for educators who believe in the importance of face-to-face learning, but recognize no matter where learning happens, teaching others about the value of human relationships, community connections, culture, and a sense of belonging for everyone are most important.

I thank my family for being supportive of my many dreams and recognizing my passion for learning is one without end. I have been blessed with amazing mentors, both in education and in life. I dedicate this book to each one of them; thank you for caring about our future teachers, students, and communities. It is my time to pay-it-forward!

Contents

Preface

This book is inspired by a promise I made to myself and others as I watched our world slowly disconnecting from itself, particularly during the past ten years. With an opportunity to teach more than 2,400 undergraduate college students during that time span, I witnessed young people lose touch with what it means to be deeply connected to friends, family, local communities, and the richness of diversity in culture, all leading to a catastrophic change in communication. I watched teachers struggle while working with parents for the sake of a child. I listened to frustrated parents talk about the lack of time and relationships with their children and their schools. I talked with organizational leaders who saw a decrease in community memberships and overall engagement. And, I spoke to workers who felt their employers really did not care about their role in the company as human beings, but rather as a means to an end.

As I spoke with and observed others, I noticed their own mounting angst was parallel to mine, and I wanted to do something about it. At that time, I was a professor at a college, so I offered to design a course in effective communication for undergraduate teacher education candidates. Though I believe the course was valuable and productive for future educators, it still did not really meet the needs and goals of a larger audience. I believe the course provided one supporting, foundational cornerstone to my ultimate goal, but I needed a ton of stones to build this house if there was to be a sense of belonging for everyone. With that said, even this book is not meant to be an all-encompassing manual, but rather a guidebook to help others gain strategies that are practical enough to make meaningful connections in their own circle of influence. If we can encourage people to interact and engage with one another to create a sense of belonging, our local communities will re-ignite with connections. Join me as I share with you what I have learned through my experiences and why we need to focus on the value of culture, the importance of community, and the essential need for communication.

Introduction

Culture. Community. Communication. These three words support human relationships and the human experience in spite of all the chaos that challenges us on a daily basis. By design, we need others in our lives. Whether we are with family, friends, colleagues, competitors, or complete strangers, we innately desire a sense of belonging in a community. We have a keen need for others to respect and value our culture. We need to see value in communication, to recognize that if we learn how to effectively express ourselves, we can communicate facts, thoughts, and emotions. We can learn how to send and receive clear messages for greater connection and less miscommunication.

Our ideas, our beliefs, and our goals will fall upon deaf ears if we cannot convey to others the undeniable need to value culture, community, and communication. We need to relay the importance behind the need to listen and understand the perspective of others, not just our own. We may never be in total agreement, but we must choose to tolerate and expand our minds (and vocabulary) if we desire to engage others in our lives, not as bystanders, but as invested participants. We all must work together to gain and maintain a vibrant culture, a cohesive community, and effective communication in today's world. We must strive for a sense of belonging in the human experience.

If we learn how to effectively communicate, committing ourselves to understanding the culture of those in our communities, <u>we can and will make a</u> difference and reach our goals.

But, how….? Well, it begins with each of us taking time to reflect on what it means to communicate with others in today's world, especially those in our school communities. We must never lose the heart and soul of who and what we are, including our heritage and our history. These are invaluable markers that show where we have traveled and build the roadmap for our future. If we do not make the time to be attentive to the details in our classroom communities, we will never know how to build upon the greatest decisions or steer away from the mistakes made by others.

We must also learn what it means to use ethos, pathos, and logos in our decision making…and to do it well. The world we live in today can be overwhelming; our best intentions can quickly become mishaps unless we focus on caring for ourselves and one another. It is a balancing act that requires a concerted commitment by each person in a school community, especially the classroom teacher.

We must never lose sight of balancing our mind, body, and spirit. We must help others do the same thing. We need to build relationships that recognize and support the importance of balance; one that will sustain a school community and its culture during tumultuous times of change. It is imperative we never lose sight of where we have been as we move forward to where we want to be. Our future success depends on us building a sense of belonging for others while focusing on what we set out to accomplish within our community.

A PLACE TO PONDER

1

What Is Your Ultimate Goal?

What are your goals for your classroom this year? What is your priority, your purpose? Is your purpose meant to inform or persuade your students about learning, life, themselves? Why should they even care about what you want to make happen this year? And how can you encourage others to be actively engaged with your goals for learning and for your classroom? How can your students trust that you see them as a valuable asset and that you are invested in their success beyond grades?

The best thing you can do right now is to think about and write down what you and your school values and believes to be most important for your students. People should be the most important part of any organization, from your leaders to your community members. If you can personally verbalize the heart and soul of your school's mission, you can determine a huge part of your purpose as a classroom teacher! You should not change the core of yourself as a teacher to please others just for the sake of having happy colleagues and students. You will only create a fractured foundation for your classroom, leading to issues when difficult events happen.

An effective way to find your purpose, mission, vision, and goals is to complete what I refer to as my *5W1H Self-Assessment*. My experiences with others led me to create this tool. You will see the self-assessment tool later in the book, so right now the goal is merely familiarizing yourself with it.

5W1H Self-Assessment

- **Who** do you want to inform, persuade, or engage in a conversation or activity? In this case, you might say students, parents, colleagues.
- **What** is your purpose as your plan to lead your classroom community?
- **Where, when,** and **how** does the mission you have for your classroom connect to your school's goal? Does it match your heart and soul goal(s) for your students?
- **Why** should students even care and want to engage with your classroom community?

You are more likely to succeed **when** you begin with your end goal in mind. It makes everyone, including yourself more confident. Clear goals help build trust in what is being said and done within an organization, no matter **where** it is happening.

What I am about to share next is crucial to remember as you work to reach any goal. <u>Culture can be productive or destructive</u>. Just one person can change the group dynamics between what could be a constructive culture or a toxic culture. This can happen with any community, no matter if it is face-to-face or online. We absolutely need to know the types of people we are dealing with; we need to be people-savvy. We must think about how we manage our time together and build a foundation that fosters productive, purposeful relationships.

<u>Think Tank Time #1</u>

- **What is your main purpose as a teacher? If asked, how would describe your classroom goals?**
- **Do you have a mission statement for your school? What about your own mission statement for your classroom community?**
- **Do you have a list of goals you hope to accomplish this year in tangible, actionable words?**

- **What words are integral and must be included in your teaching mission statement or vision statement? Take the time to not only list them but provide solid evidence for their value.**

Write down your goal and mission, say them aloud, role play by sharing them with your inner circle of colleagues prior to broadcasting them out to your students. It is not too soon to start thinking strategically about your plans. Here are a few questions to get you started. You will see these later in the book, as well.

YOUR STRATEGIC PLANNING GUIDE

1. **What about your school and mission matches what matters to your students and your local community?**
2. **What is the purpose of your job as a teacher? What matters most to your students?**
3. **Is your primary goal to inform, to persuade, or to evoke participation?**
4. **Are you hoping to inspire your students in such a way that they will pay attention and listen so they can understand new information and community goals?**

5. **Are you looking to build a case of persuasion to have them agree with you and/or disagree with other points of view or ideas in your classroom?**
6. **Is your goal to encourage others to engage/take part in your classroom or to meet a goal?**

Do not worry about having all the answers right now. The goal is to work through each question by gaining understanding first, then applying what you learned later. Eventually, you will build a timeline to gauge, plan, and create your strategic action steps with tangible assessments to determine your success. There are several ways to design strategic classroom community plans for success and I have supplied two examples on this book's online partner site at www.whybalancematters.com. Of course, there are numerous checkpoints along the way with either plan to determine how things are progressing. These are best managed by the most objective and purposeful people in your circle of influence, your mentor colleagues and of course, your students. It is also important to remember...sometimes, plans change...that is why we have checkpoints. We want to keep the train moving forward, not derailing because we rushed the process.

Human nature pushes us to determine what matters most when dealing with every decision in life. As you think about your classroom, ask yourself these three questions, <u>not from your perspective</u>, but from that of the students in your community that are part of your target audience.

Think Tank Time #2

- **What makes _____ important enough for my time and attention?**
- **Why should I care about _____?**
- **Will I support or not support _____ this purpose?**

I know there are tons of questions heading your way right now about what the future looks like, but if you can proactively spot potential problems now, you can plan ahead and minimize or even eliminate many of those problems ahead of time. Be sure you have someone who is unbiased to help you clearly see your goals and roadblocks. Be consistently proactive in planning ahead. Check out chapter seven for more information.

2

To Inform or Persuade?

Today, even with all our advancements in communication, there is still much that can be learned from history. Around 4 B.C., there lived a great philosopher and teacher named Aristotle. He studied under Plato, tutored Alexander the Great, and authored over 200 writings, one of which was titled *Rhetoric*. Today, rhetoric is still very much alive and relevant. Rhetoric is the principle of training communicators to inform or persuade.

Aristotle's Art of Persuasion

Ethos	• Understanding with Perspective • Persuade with Positivity • Speak with Credibility and Character
Pathos	• Awareness of Perception of Supporters/Adversaries • Open-Minded to Tolerance, Not Acceptance • Personable with Supporters/Adversaries
Logos	• Purpose • Clear Communication • Decision-Making

Ethos, Pathos, Logos

Ethos is the appeal to the ethics of others. Ethics are moral principles that determine a person's behavior. The goal of ethos is to convince an audience that you are legitimately credible and of good character. It is really all about you making an impact on your audience. If they believe that you are honestly sharing information, persuasively or not, they will find value and support you. If the moral principles of an individual/community can be persuaded to believe what you present, then they will find it worthy of their time and attention. In my experience, ethos is most successful if you emphasize an understanding of another person's perspective, persuade with positivity about what works best, and speak with character and credible information.

Pathos is an appeal to the emotions of others. The goal of pathos is having the ability to present/persuade in a way that makes gut connections with an individual/community. It causes an audience to have a sense of "this is important to me, even if I can't explain why right now" and convinces them to be active in their engagement with an activity or within a community. A crucial point to remember is an individual's beliefs and values (ethics) affect their emotions. They may <u>choose to not make</u> a connection to the people involved within the group if they have a strong moral conviction. This is where you may have heard, "No matter what, always let your conscience be your guide". Of the three areas of Aristotle's model, <u>pathos can be the most volatile</u>, as it is completely up to each person's emotional attachment or detachment with a group and/or any given idea. Often, the most passionate supporters or adamant adversaries are impacted by pathos. If you want to be most successful in the area of pathos, you must emphasize an awareness of perceptions, an open mind to tolerate (not necessarily accept) the thoughts of others, and be personable with both supporters and adversaries.

Logos is an appeal to the logical part of the mind. The goal of using logos is to present information in a logical, clearly communicated manner that makes it easiest for others to comprehend and understand. If people are able to evaluate the information shared, analyzing it to determine if makes sense because of the reasoning behind the purpose, then you have met the goals of logos. You must provide key information, an argument with tangible persuasion and a plan of action, and a sense that whatever is being asked is the right thing to do based on the information provided at the time. It is important to remember that logos is tied to the information at hand, not the people delivering the information. Emotions do not usually come into play at all. If you want to most successful in the area of logos, you must emphasize <u>importance of purpose, clear communication, and decision-making!</u>

The following questions are to help guide you as we move into the next chapter on culture. Do not answer them right now. (I will remind you when to respond to them and they are shared again near the end of the book.)

<u>Think Tank Time #3</u>

- **How will you emphasize the importance of relationships in your plan to engage others?**
- **How will you effectively communicate your purpose with those in your community of learners?**
- **What do you feel will work best when persuading others to become engaged with your classroom community?**

3

Culture and Community

What is Culture?

Culture is a 'way of life'. It is built upon how groups of people do things. Read that again…it is based on how <u>people do things</u>! Culture includes our attitudes, beliefs, values, standards, traditions…all things we defend to be true and right. We demonstrate our culture through our behavior. It is not something we can easily control. In today's world, we are given seemingly endless opportunities to express ourselves by what we do, not just what we say! Honestly, we should have no trouble engaging students in our classrooms. What is one tool that we have that promotes our sharing of our attitudes, beliefs, and values more than ever before. That's right, technology!

Yet, we must be keenly aware of its shortcomings and dangers. Technology allows us to express ourselves without much thought and introspection. We can express tolerance or hate in seconds, with just one post. Once we click send, the damage is done. We must be responsible for our actions. Technology provides us a platform to hate and shame others who do not conform to our ideals. It can be a battle of good vs. evil with every post shared. It can destroy or build individuals and communities. However, we can also learn more about ourselves and others. We can represent and defend who and what we believe, collaborating with others to build credibility and community. We must recognize technology has given us the ability to destroy or build communities, especially those in our classrooms and schools. Most importantly, we must know that whatever we share online will always be found, no matter how far into cyberspace we send it. It will never disappear once it is posted. Keep this in mind…always! Tell others the same thing.

BUILD RELATIONSHIPS

FOCUS ON CULTURE and COMMUNITY

Do your research ahead of time...**get to know your audience**!

How can you build relationships to connect people, even at a distance?

Use available resources, harness technology for your purpose!

Our culture is tied to how and why we form or join communities, both personally and professionally. Just like technology today, culture has historically been productive or destructive. Just one person can make a difference in what could be a constructive culture or a toxic culture in any community. You need to be people-savvy and effectively communicate what you believe to be right but do it with tolerance. No matter the communication platform, if you disagree, you need to communicate with **poise, professionalism, and reflection**. These three skills are fundamental if you want to successfully interact with others.

As we learn the value and skillset of poise, professionalism, and reflection, we must set goals to teach others. We must teach these skills in our homes, schools, and organizations. It is not optional! We must gain and maintain poise in the face of adversity, gain and maintain professionalism, and actively reflect on decisions so we learn from our mistakes. Learning these three skills does not happen overnight. It takes good leadership, consistent modeling, and constructive criticism within our circle of influence. It takes commitment!

What is Community?

When you think about community, what comes to mind? Do you think of a place where you live or work? Do you think of a school or a college campus? Many businesses have the word *community* built into their names. What about the name of a housing complex or a retirement home? You might even live or work at a place with the word "community" in its name. Well, does being part of a community mean anything special to you? Do you feel like you truly belong there? Do you feel a connection with those in the group?

Historically, the word 'community' ties together people living in an area with common interests. The Latin roots of the word **community** include "public spirit, shared in common." Communities are social units with commonalities in norms and values. Communities have deep cultural connections, often tied to beliefs, traditions, and values from the past.

School communities create ongoing opportunities for an individual or group to gain followers. The philosopher, Aristotle, spoke about emotions often being enough to earn "buy in and engagement" from others. Just think, historically, families picked a certain place to live, raise a family, work, worship, and play based on the community they felt most connected with. Places where they could fellowship and contribute to the greater good because everyone shared the same beliefs. As time passed, families and communities grew in population. This led to continued opportunities for growth within the community of shared beliefs and values, leading to them extending beyond the immediate geographic location.

THE VALUE OF CULTURE and COMMUNITY

DESCRIBE YOUR SCHOOL'S CULTURE and COMMUNITY. PEOPLE FIRST, THEN AS LEARNERS (BOTH F2F and ONLINE)

HOW WOULD SOMEONE ELSE DESCRIBE THE CULTURE AND COMMUNITY IN YOUR SCHOOL?

As we look at class reunions and alumni social media groups, we can appreciate how the educational institutions cultivated common culture and interests. They often bring people back together after many years. Shared experiences create a sense of commitment and trust. A sense of belonging and commitment to family and friends build a strong community in your classroom…and beyond.

If we are invested in growing our school communities, we must be willing to find the answers to the following questions:

- **How difficult is it for students to create a sense of community in our SCHOOL??**
- **What do students think about OUR SCHOOL'S CULTURE?**
- **What can you do to help students build a community in your classroom?**
- **How can you foster student relationships honoring culture?**

As communities continue to grow, students move from classroom to classroom, building to building, and even well beyond local geographic areas, we can encourage people to come together, continuing to engage in sharing common interests and needs. One tool that most people are using today is technology, particularly social media. Virtual communities seem like a practical choice, but they should not replace face-to-face interactions. (Before some of you stop reading, hear me out!) People cite a lack of time as their main reason for joining online communities, but we need to be cautious about what we lose when we attempt to save time. Relying on technology as a replacement for face-to-face meetings is counterproductive and dangerous. Online community spaces are unable to create deeply authentic emotional connections that are long-lasting and substantial. We eventually find an intense need to meet our online friends, often discovering the relationships built are only superficial and not clearly honest. Humans, by design, need to be nurtured at all levels of Maslow's *Hierarchy of Needs*. A sense of safety, belonging, and trust are essential.

Though technology may supplement and help support established relationships, it cannot replace a physical classroom location that fosters trust and fundamental relationships. We lose that deep commitment and sense of loyalty if we solely rely on online classroom communities, particularly with our younger students. This is one reason it is so important to recognize the value and purpose of what local brick and mortar schools offer to our students. It should compel all of us to make it a priority to find time to be available to engage with others at a physical location. We cannot have a groundbreaking ceremony for any project (building or community) without solid, physical connections.

Working Together

Culture and community are what makes a school community thrive, not merely survive. Carve out time to research and learn more about ancient civilizations, religions and churches, and multiple forms of government. Some have completely disappeared while others withstood war, famine, disease, and natural disasters. Why? They recognized that they could survive, even the harshest of conditions, if their culture and community remained strong. Today we call this sustainability.

If we want sustainability in our communities, we need to invest in people, especially young people. Students are the future leaders of our communities. We need to focus on educating our youth and young adults about the value of culture and communication. Many high school students say they cannot wait to grow up, graduate, and leave their hometown. "There is nothing here to do, and no one really cares about what we think." College student are heard saying, "I want to get away from where I grew up...people are not progressive enough in my hometown. I need to see the real world, meet new people, and find **my** place in this world."

What has made our next generation of community members feel like they are not able to make connections, find their place, and plant their roots into the soil of their childhood homes? Have we really become a wasteland of "has-been" communities with organizations with little to no value to or impact on the next generation? What is causing us to lose our sense of culture and community? Have our hometown school communities simply become holding pens for learning with no sense of belonging? We need them to see why soil beneath their feet will sustain them best during times of despair. They need to recognize that no virtual, online community can support, protect, and sustain them as much as a local classroom community.

It is obvious that many of our long-standing educational institutions are running lower on student enrollment and funds because people say they have better options, they lack interest, or don't feel a vested commitment in local schools. Many people are not even able to recall the mission, mascot, or name of their child's school building!

We need to find what makes people want to commit time and energy into their communities and schools. What makes students feel special and worthy of attention and service...and how can we highlight their importance to others? Today, the world is a melting pot of many cultures. We need to creatively think about how we can encourage our educational community to embrace this.

What can we do to reconnect with students and families? How can we get our younger generations to want to be involved, to move back home or make a new home, investing time and energy into their local communities and schools? Who says you cannot build something new that has connected value and committed interest from people in your community? We need to think more about putting people first...and then do everything possible to make it a success! What can make your students feel invested in your classrooms this academic year?

What Do Students Value?

Human relationships are what matter most. They create the culture of our communities, so we need to continually reflect on what community members value. We must not only ask the following questions, but we need to research and find evidence that supports their responses. We need to gain greater clarity about the culture and community in our local schools to gain and maintain growth within our school communities and our classrooms.

CREATE AN INVITING LEARNING ENVIRONMENT

CREATE YOUR OWN STORY!

What do students see? Hear? Feel?

What makes your classroom a great place to learn?

What can you improve on as you design your classroom community for this upcoming school year?

Here are four important questions to ask:

Think Tank Time #4

- **What appeals to your students and their families?**
- **How can you affect them in a way that they want to be a part of your classroom community and mission?**
- **What are the goals, norms, values, believes, attitudes, traditions in your classroom?**
- **What is the center of your classroom community's culture?**

Harnessing Technology

Digital communities provide "any time, any place", 24/7 availability. Physical locations are able to provide an authentic, human-necessary sense of belonging. What does this mean for the future of face-to-face, physical space classroom communities? <u>It means we need to control technology, not allow it to control us.</u> We need to become better educated about what technology honestly can and cannot do. We need to recognize its shortcomings and determine what is best in each situation. Do not use a one-size-fits-all approach.

We should think of technology as our workhorse, one we harness to cultivate relationships in the digital landscape and as a laborer who helps us augment our established, authentic school communities. The power of technology is a tool to engage group members between events and activities when we are not able to physically meet with others in our organization. *We must never let ourselves become the passenger in a vehicle driven solely by technology. No matter how "smart" others say it will become, <u>technology should never replace the human mind, body, and spirit.</u>*

If you want any organization to thrive, including your classroom, you need to focus on creating and maintaining a sense of belonging with each student. A face-to-face setting is the place where people feel valued, engaged, and understood. As you meet, you are planting seeds of growth, nurturing young sprouts and seedlings. As the relationship grow stronger, we can cultivate and supplement our communities by using technology as a workhorse to continue productive growth with others.

Do not forget to commit to finding balance both in-person and at-a-distance. Too much of one resource could cause an imbalance and your classroom community will never reach its potential growth, it may even fracture and crumble. Always being aware of the original mission and vision for your classroom and school. Your vision must drive technology, technology must never drive your vision. This may seem foreign to our younger generation of teachers, who have not had an opportunity to see the value of meeting face-to- face, as technology has been pushed to replace it in all facets of their lives. The childhood lifestyle of our youth has emphasized the power of technology to bring connections with others, to learn, to communicate. Use it as a catalyst to grow communities of significance in your classroom.

As mentioned before, an imbalance in resources can cause chaos. There is evidence that technology plays a significant role in mental health and the crisis we are facing with our youth today. Many of our students have never had a genuine sense of belonging, which is innately part of how we are designed as humans. We must be certain they see value in face-to-face relationships and that we see value in each one of them.

Technology has increased the amount and type of communication we use each day. This sounds like it would make all communities stronger. But we must look more deeply. This means we need to learn how to effectively communicate using technology to gain and support our connections. When someone accept a social media friend request from you, "likes" what you post, or comments on what you say, you feel valued in some way. If we get our posts "shared" with others, that must mean we are super important, right? At least for the ten seconds as someone scrolls past what was shared. Many people do not recognize just how shallow these forms of communication are in the big scheme of things.

The human body, particularly the brain desires to connect, to belong, somewhere with something…in some cases, anywhere with anything. It is a sad reality that many students only receive acceptance or approval in a virtual world. Individuals, families, and organizations need to recognize this problem and work collectively together to confront it. We need to emphasize how authentic in-person relationships offer a greater sense of value, commitment, and community building, unlike superficial, fleeting online experiences.

For our youth, instant feedback from others is something they expect to receive and give, often without much thought. Just that statement alone demonstrates the intense need for us to talk about the importance of quality, effective communication. We need to focus on spending time with children and teens, using face-to-face communication skills, teaching patience, problem-solving, respect, manners, and kindness. They should also be taught how to apply these things as they communicate at-a-distance online. Youth need to understand that long-distance kudos and criticism can lack genuine commitment, are often superficial, with many not lasting beyond the moment it was shared online.

Social media has made it so easy for students to change their perspective and opinions based on emotions and the influence of others. They see people who are jumping from one group to another, following and unfollowing in an instant, without any conscience or consequence. It is easy to step away from a group when you have no physical investment and fade away into the cyber sunset without much reflection or repercussion. This leads to a lack of responsibility. Think about how quickly you can like or unlike, follow or unfollow someone online? Online relationships lack a true sense of belonging and critical thinking.

We need to show how important a sense of belonging is to our physical, mental, and social well-being. Remember connecting with others is how we continue to build upon *Maslow's Hierarchy of Needs*. If we build upon a virtual sense of belonging and it vanishes, we lose faith and trust in those relationships that may be genuine in the future. A lack of trust is a basic need that must be fulfilled, or further healthy growth is not possible. If we lose trust in others, we lose our desire to engage with others. We lose a sense of belonging, which can lead to devastating choices and consequences. This is a direct connection to our mental health crisis today.

Education is powerful. We must educate ourselves and others that joining an online group or social network does not require the same type of emotional investment, nor does it give the same type of emotional return as real human interaction, especially at a local community level. Step back and look at the hierarchy of any successful, long-standing organization. It will usually have a national headquarters with regional, state, and local affiliates. The same holds true for federal, state, and local government. Even within our educational system, each individual state is able to determine a certain percentage of what is taught in a school's curriculum based on the culture and local history of its community. Think about it…local, in-person communities do indeed matter! It may be the one thing that saves humanity and helps fight against our mental health crisis. If we invest in others, others will invest in us!

If we want to keep our educational institutions thriving, our teachers invested in one another, our youth connected with true reality, not augmented reality, we need to study and invest in our local communities, including your classrooms. We need to focus on providing opportunities for students to engage in human experience with "hands-on, minds-on" activities that bolster our physiological and emotional well-being. If we do so, students will see the value of reinvesting in physical spaces with material resources being used as the glue that holds us to one another until we meet face-to-face again. Technology is a valuable tool in today's world; however, it is not the "end-all, be-all" of how we communicate with one another.

No matter what community we may find ourselves a part of, we must learn to choose the most effective strategies to communicate. This is essential if we want to build human relationships that harness technology and social media to enhance, but certainly not replace the human experience. Face-to-face relationships are fundamental to fostering culture, community, and communication.

In an earlier chapter, I supplied "Think Tank Time" questions, and I told you that you would see them again. Take time right now to answer the questions before moving forward in the book.

Think Tank Time #3 (Revisited)

- **How will you emphasize the importance of relationships in your plan to engage others?**
- **How will you effectively communicate your purpose with those in your community of learners?**

- **What do you feel will work best when persuading others to become engaged with your classroom community?**

A PLACE TO PONDER

4

Let's Talk about Communication

What is Communication?

Communication is the exchange of information. It is a means of sending or receiving information. From cave drawings to debate, papyrus scrolls to digital paper, from typewriters to texting, we have found ways to share information with others. The need to communicate is built into our DNA. We want to connect with others! The use of verbal, nonverbal, written, and visual types of communication are the four most traditional forms of communication in our world. Depending on our age and our culture, certain people are more adept at using several types of communication. Being effective and efficient with multiple communication pathways is critical to developing a sense of community today. Therefore, I believe people watching is essential in today's world.

Not only do our words speak volumes, but the power of body language is incredibly important. If our goal is to create a community of engagement and sense of belonging in our classrooms, we must pay close attention to everything we "say" without words. Honestly, our non-verbal body language is often more telling and genuine than any other type of communication.

With that said, take a few minutes right now to reflect on how you prefer to communicate and why you find certain types of communication challenging. It will help you become aware of what challenges you may face as you work to reach your goals.

<u>PERSONAL QUIZ</u>

(There are no right or wrong answers!)

How do you prefer to communicate with others (verbal, nonverbal, written, and visual)? Why?

How do you prefer <u>not to</u> communicate with others (verbal, nonverbal, written, and visual)? Why?

What is your biggest challenge when communicating with others?

Why Communicate?

What makes communication important? What is its' purpose in our lives? We use communication much like Aristotle used ethos, pathos, and logos. We want to inform others, to encourage others to think for themselves, not merely follow the majority. We want to express emotions and feelings. We want to influence and persuade. And most importantly, we want to be social! Yet, each day we have people sending unclear messages. These miscommunications lead to mistakes with products, services, and relationships.

Communication Choices

With so many new forms of communications, we have not learned how to engage effectively in today's world Professionally and personally, we still have not become savvy enough to leverage these new forms of communication to our advantage. We listen to what others tell us to do, but we rarely take time to think if it is the best tool for the job. Unfortunately, we are no longer teaching traditional communication strategies that are still relevant and essential. For example, we are repeating history by using cave-like drawings and hieroglyphics as our modern day emojis! (Which I do like a lot, but they are not the best communication tool.) As we keep adding new tools, we are deleting the fundamental skillset of effective communication. Deciding on the right tool for any job requires skill and purposeful planning.

Communication with technology has allowed us to respond so quickly that we often create more problems than good as we muddy our messages with half-written words and incomplete thoughts. We need to emphasize the importance of drafting and revising, committing to "say what we intend before we hit send". We can and must do a better job with this. We can host short workshop trainings, practice roleplaying scenario responses to help others gain this skill.

We need to continually practice as technology evolves. Efficiency does not equate to effectiveness. The good news is that traditional forms of communication and social media each use the same foundation of sending and receiving messages. If we can learn to employ the same strategies across both platforms, effective communication can happen.

We must decide to be the leaders of this communication revival. Without us, it will not happen! We are only one generation away from losing the 'language' of authentic traditional communication. As teachers, we are the last hope for effective communication.

Think Tank Time #5

Thinking about effective communication...

- **How can you effectively communicate and share information with a larger audience in your local community to encourage participation in your school and classroom?**

- **How can you create opportunities for students to learn how to effectively communicate?**

~~~~

What is Effective Communication?

Effective communication is not impossible, it is not even difficult once you focus on gaining and maintaining the necessary skills and awareness of others in the conversation. It is not rocket science, nor does it require an advanced degree. Effective communication requires an understanding of how messages are sent and received, much like radio waves and wi-fi signals today. No matter what message we send, there is always a sender and a receiver. If we are the sender, then we want to be sure our messages are clear, concise, and purposeful. We want to encourage open communication by sending a message that compels the receiver to either respond in word or action. If the message is clearly articulated prior to being sent, there is only one thing that can lead to its miscommunication: interference. We will talk about interference in a little while, but first let us discuss the construction of any intended message.

Sending Messages

As the sender, we must think about why we are beginning the conversation prior to starting it. What is our purpose? Recognize I am not talking about small talk, but conversation related to an already planned focus. What makes the need for this conversation important? Just as a writer needs to know his/her audience, a leader should be prepared and know his/her audience. This is where the power of words becomes important. Word choice based on audience and culture, sentence structure, and tone are all items that should be determined and accurately used prior to sending a message.

Think about and determine the following before you move on with any communication if you want to be most effective and efficient:

- Who is the intended audience?
- What is the purpose for sending the message?
- What is your perspective and how can you best ensure your message is clearly shared with them?
- What have you done to encourage open communication in your message?
- Is there a response you are hoping to gain from your communication?
- What do you think the intended receiver's reaction may be to the message you are sending?
- What happens if you do not get back the message from the receiver you had hoped for?
- What might be a roadblock to your planned communication with this audience?
- What can you do to mitigate that roadblock?
- Does the message you are sending show that you value the receiver as an individual without compromising your own intended message or purpose?
- If it does not, is there valid reasoning that you are sending your message without valuing the receiver as a person? (Remember, you can dislike a behavior without disliking the person!)

Receiving Messages

Being the receiver of a message, especially if it is unexpected, can create anxiety and emotion. Hopefully, the message sent is clear and direct, with an opportunity for interaction tied to a purposeful response or action. We must be aware of interference at this point. Just like static on the radio or a lost signal or phone call, we may only be picking up pieces of the intended message, no matter how well planned it was when it was originally sent. However, if there is no interference or bias present from others, we should receive an objective response, focusing on the purpose of the message, not merely the people who sent the message.

Human relationships are essential and recognizing emotions is important, but we must stay focused on a purpose to remain objective. It will allow productive work to be completed efficiently and without emotional stress. If it is not possible, we must be patient and ask for clarification, mitigating potential emotional distress prior to jumping to conclusions.

Once we read and understand the message received, we switch roles and now become the sender. A similar set of questions like those just shared becomes our responsibility.

- What is your response to the sender based on? Ethos, pathos, logos?
- What is your perspective and how can you best ensure your message is clearly shared with the original sender?
- What have you done to encourage continued open communication in your response?
- Is there a response you are hoping to gain back from your communication?
- What do you think the initial messenger's reaction may be to the response you are sending?
- What happens if you do not get back the response from the initial messenger you had hoped for?
- What might be a roadblock to your planned communication with this audience?
- What can you do to mitigate that roadblock?
- Does the message you are sending show that you value the other person as an individual without compromising your own intended message or purpose?

- If it does not, is there valid reasoning that you are sending your message without valuing the other person? (Remember, you can disapprove of a behavior without disapproving the person!)

Message Interference

No matter what, there will always be some form of interference when communicating. The goal is to minimize the noise without creating more interference. Hyper-analysis, prejudice, and anxiety can create message interference. Remember, interference can be self-created. Superfluous information, word choice, sentence length and structure, tone, and body language can all lead to noise interference…and miscommunication.

We may experience interference caused by others. Sometimes this can be even purposeful interference by others. They may intentionally sabotage the original message and skew its intended purpose. The latter is where almost every problem occurs due to a lack of perspective and respect for the individuals involved. This specifically connects to ethos, pathos, and logos. You may find just asking clarification questions without insinuating disrespect works well in this type of situation. Things may be written unclearly, without enough direction or focus, causing emotions to flare due to misunderstandings or intentional aggravation. Work to minimize these interferences as you receive and send messages.

If you sense you are becoming agitated by the other person or group, take time to gather your thoughts before responding. You can easily "talk to yourself" rather than sharing your angst with others. If you are unsure about the clarity of your response, share it with those in your inner circle. Consider not saying something unless it is beneficial to the conversation and issue being discussed at that time.

Words are incredibly powerful! They can cut deeply, especially those used with anger and malice. Sometimes we unintentionally say things and cause problems. A word of advice: if this happens, immediately step forward and rectify what has been miscommunicated. Otherwise, a loss of trust and a sense of community might become irreparably damaged. Unfortunately, relationships end because of miscommunication. Minimize the interference to maximize relationships.

Final Thoughts

Remember that what we say is as important as how we say it. We can best communicate with others if we send clear messages that are purposeful and prompt. Effective and efficient communication is essential if we want to encourage communities to grow and prosper as they work together to reach their goals. We must use all forms of communication, including body language to create a sense of trust and belonging, even in the face of disagreement. By doing so, we can agree to disagree and still hold one another in high esteem. No community will have agreement 100% of the time, but if we respect one another, we will accomplish remarkable things and prosper. Communication matters! As a teacher, you are the leader of this communication success or failure.

5

Face It,

Put People First

As much as we integrate the use of technology and revel in having so many options when it comes to connecting with others, we must not forget our essential human need for trust and faith in one another. We live in a world that requires human interaction, yet we are unknowingly allowing ourselves to disconnect from authentic human relationships. As we tally up our superficial friends, even as we say we are connected to hundreds of others, supposedly just like us, we are lonelier than ever. Recent events have supplied solid evidence of just how much we need our local communities and human connections.

Perceptions and Perspectives

Two things to always be aware of when it comes to interacting with our others are perceptions and perspectives. Do you know the difference between perceptions and perspectives? Perceptions are what people believe to be true based on their senses and experiences. Perspectives are what are created from those perceptions, including shared experiences and beliefs of others. When we take those words and tie them to education, a whole new perspective appears for each person.

As you think about your own schooling and then your classroom, think about this:

- How do perceptions turn into perspectives?
- What role do perceptions play in building a sense of community?
- What can we do as teachers to have students develop positive perspectives for learning and relationships?

HOW CAN WE CREATE CLASSROOM COMMUNITIES?

PUT STUDENTS FIRST

BUILD RELATIONSHIPS

CREATE AN INVITING LEARNING ENVIRONMENT

Think Tank Time #6

- **What could be problems or interferences you may face when sharing your classroom mission, vision, and planned activities?**
- **How can you be most clear in communicating with your students and families?**
- **What about those who are not supporting your goals? How will you address them in a professional manner?**

One of the statements I use quite often is:

"Prepare for the worst, but plan for the best."

What does this mean? I believe it means to think ahead and prepare for as many roadblocks and challenges as possible that <u>could</u> happen and then create solutions for each one. In addition, you always keep planning with your end goal in mind for the best end scenario possible. We need to reflect on our expectations as an opportunity to build a connected community of learners.

I often get asked the following big question by teachers:

Attitude is so important when you are working to build a sense of culture and community in any organization. If you are the leader, you must lead with assertive positivity. You must be enthusiastic about the future possibilities for success within your classroom and school. If you do not believe in your own mission, how can you expect others to buy-in and support your mission and vision?

Take time right now to jot down your ideas about your role as a classroom teacher and how your role impacts the culture and community in your classroom. Reflect on both face-to-face (F2F) and online expectations you have for your classroom.

YOUR ROLE AS THE TEACHER

DESCRIBE YOUR TEACHING PHILOSOPHY

LIST YOUR EXPECTATIONS FOR YOUR
CLASSROOM
(BOTH F2F and ONLINE)

Ask yourself:

- What makes your teaching philosophy special for students?

- What are you doing as a teacher to create a sense of community in your classes?

- What are you doing as a teacher to foster a sense of belonging for all your students? Explain.

- How do you know students feel safe to learn with you as their teacher?

The next step is to think about your students. First, and foremost, they are human beings. Therefore, think of them as people and what you know about people their age. Describe them using all your senses and knowledge. Be cognizant of your own perceptions and perspective. Be open-minded and aware about their culture and communities outside of your classroom.

THE ROLE OF YOUR STUDENTS

DESCRIBE YOUR STUDENTS
AS PEOPLE FIRST, THEN AS LEARNERS

(BOTH F2F and ONLINE)

Ask yourself the following questions:

- What makes your students challenging to teach?
- How difficult is it for students to create a sense of community in your classroom??
- What do your students need to feel a sense of belonging?
- What can your students do to build a community in your classroom?
- How can you foster student relationships to happen and teach content?

Remember, humans innately need a sense of belonging to be complete and whole. Take the time to reflect on our mental health crisis and you will find people who do not have a true sense of belonging, lack authentic face-to-face connections with others, and have little sense of reality. Yet, they may still have an active social media presence. We need to look more closely at mental health from this perspective and the negative impact technology may be having on the human experience. We need to focus on fostering a sense of belonging in this world and why culture, community, and communication are critical parts of our society. These three areas are where we need to focus our attention and invest funding for research. The impact we make in this world starts with how we manage our educational institutions, our classroom communities, and most importantly, ourselves.

Maslow's Hierarchy of Needs

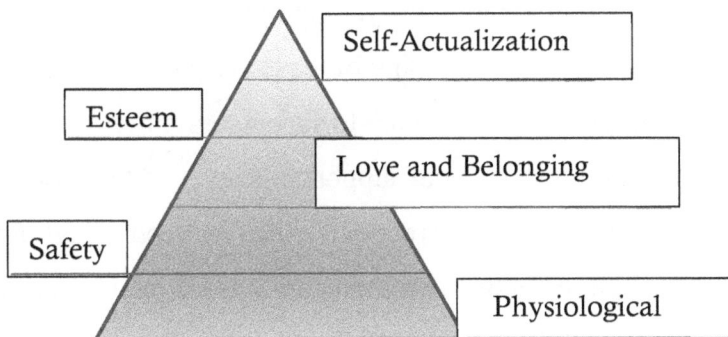

We can strive for any goal we want in our lives, but if we do not have access to resources that support our fundamental needs of mind, body and spirit, we will never attain our fullest potential or self-actualization. Maslow's *Hierarchy of Needs* is invaluable if you value people. Abraham Maslow was a psychologist who focused on what humans need to be fulfilled, categorizing their needs into five distinct levels.

Firstly, essential physiology needs must be met for basic life to be sustainable (air, water, food, shelter, sleep, clothing). These are needs that can only be met in an actual physical location, where tangible resources are available. These include food supplies, physical shelter to sleep, and clothing to protect us from the natural elements of weather.

Secondly, Maslow identifies the essential need for safety (personal security, employment, resources, health, property). Again, many of these are physical needs that are only provided from face-to-face interactions. While technology may help support this level of Maslow's hierarchy, we must recognize that we need actual physical spaces. Effective communication is critically important at this level. It can foster or fracture our access to employment, resources, healthcare, and property. As a community, we must emphasize the importance of relationship building and sense of security. We must build trust in our places of employment. Many people spend more time working with others each day than spending time with their own families. Human relationships must be recognized as fundamental determiners of success.

If a person is able to have physiological and safety needs met, they can reach the third level of Maslow's hierarchy. This level focuses on loving and belonging (a sense of connection). If we aspire to have others invest in our educational institutions and our classroom community's work, then this is the level we must create opportunities for engagement and value. So many people are seeking a sense of connection. We must recognize that students are turning to online virtual communities in an attempt to fulfill this need. We have become so busy with life that students feel that they are unable to find time to make authentic, face-to-face connections with others outside of work. Yet, by human design, we need to find our place in this world by connecting with others.

A keen sense of community is part of each student's being. As a classroom leader, you must focus an enormous amount of time and energy at this level or you will not be able to get others to engage, connect, and commit to your classroom community. If you want to reach beyond the day-to-day challenges of surviving and striving, you must place emphasis on connecting and engaging people in your circle of influence…and beyond.

Once a person has a sense of belonging and trust with others, they will be able to focus on Maslow's fourth level, which is esteem (respect, self-esteem status, recognition). Our youth find themselves ill-equipped to deal with the constant onslaught of social media. It has a negative impact on their self-esteem, self-respect, social respect, and status. Years ago, we had an opportunity to hear different perspectives and voices to be or leave behind when we left school, work, or family. Today, the noise is constant and can be overwhelming, unending buzz of negativity. Mental health organizations need to take the time to not only call upon medical doctor, psychiatrists, and counselors, but they should hone in on this area of Maslow's hierarchy. We should have a task force in each community to determine how to best address this issue, with not only our youngest, most vulnerable population of developing minds, but also our adult population. People matter!

Lastly, the ultimate level of Maslow's *Hierarchy of Needs* is self-actualization, a place where humans have an opportunity to employ all available resources and talents to not only survive, but to totally thrive. If we want our children, our family, friends, colleagues, employees, leaders, and ourselves to reach our fullest potential, using our unique talents, we must recognize, address, and foster ALL levels of Maslow's *Hierarchy of Needs*. We must commit to integrating this hierarchy into our classroom and within our own lives. We need to integrate this hierarchy into our day-to-day activities to balance the power of the human mind, body, and spirit.

A PLACE TO PONDER

6

How People Connect

Once our fundamental physiological and safety needs are met, we begin to make decisions about who and what we desire to make connections with, engage in activities with, and where we choose to commit our time and energy. A community is where more than two people choose to gather. What do students choose to do? Students make choices based on where they think they fit in.

Human nature leads us to use our senses. Visually, what we see makes an impact on our decisions. It may not be an accurate representation of what is real, but what we perceive is right is what matters to us. There can be a lot of misconceptions because what we view from a distance can easily be distorted. We must remember the importance of perceptions and watch out for misrepresentations.

In addition, how we communicate non-verbally through our actions is certainly one of the most defining way we communicate. It is often hard to hide our emotions. Our actions and reactions speak much louder than our words. When we do speak, what others hear (or perceive they hear) also makes an impact. This is known as our verbal communication. Our word choice, tone, level, speed, and oral expression all convey our voice. Even our non-verbal communication can be "heard". Our tone and pitch are those "actions" that speak louder than words.

Both are equally important, so we need to reflect on how we communicate both verbally and non-verbally, in person and at a distance. We must not only be aware of other people's feelings, but we should recognize what their perceptions of us mean to our community.

Beliefs can turn into perspectives, which can become deeply embedded into a culture, often for extended periods of time. People, including students, make decisions about what they find credible or fake based on perspectives that others share. Emotional connections and understanding can lead to disagreements or support by others. Perceptions, perspectives, emotions, facts vs opinions, and purpose…all have clear connections to Aristotle's use of ethos, pathos, and logos.

If you recall in chapter two, we discussed how Aristotle authored the art of persuasion, including the appeals of *ethos, pathos, and logos* around 4 B.C. His ultimate goal was to get whatever he wanted through persuasion. Debate and discussion were indispensable during that time period. Aristotle's use of ethos, pathos, and logos still affect how we connect and communicate with people. Time well spent "people watching" prior to employing ethos, pathos, or logos with a classroom community is essential. People watching allows us to work smarter, not harder. It allows us to determine the best way to connect with and engage our community members, so they choose to commit their time and energy toward a common goal.

BUILD A SENSE OF BELONGING IN YOUR CLASSROOM

KNOW YOUR STUDENTS

BUILD YOUR OWN CLASSROOM STORY

DETERMINE THE 5 W's and H?
Who, what, when, where, why and how?

MAKE YOUR CLASSROOM A COMMUNITY FOR ALL!

Rebecca J Speelman, LLC

Think about it: human nature helps us determine what matters most...with every decision in life.

Think Tank Time #2 (Revisited)

We subconsciously ask these three questions with each decision:

- **What makes _____ important enough for my time and attention?**
- **Why should I care about _____?**
- **Will I support or not support _____ this purpose?**

So, what do you expect the responses will be when you share these three bullet points with your students and your colleagues?   Attempt to not prejudge anyone based on what others may told you, as these are only perceived as truth. Gain your own perspective. Make your own decisions. Be authentic!

IT'S TIME TO WORK:

PUTTING YOUR IDEAS
INTO ACTION

YOUR STRATEGIC PLANNING GUIDE

Write down your answers to these questions.

1. What about your school and mission matches what matters to your students and your local community?
2. What is the purpose of your job as a teacher? What matters most to your students?
3. Is your primary goal to inform, to persuade, or to evoke participation?
4. Are you hoping to inspire your students in such a way that they will pay attention and listen so they can understand new information and community goals?
5. Are you looking to build a case of persuasion to have them agree with you and/or disagree with other points of view or ideas in your classroom?
6. Is your goal to encourage others to engage/participate in your classroom or to meet a goal?

7

Strategies for Success

How can you effectively communicate in today's world, recognizing the value of your classroom community's culture and seeking the best strategies to engage all students?

~~~

Strategic Tip #1:

First things first, you need to do your own hometown community research. Get ready to start super sleuthing for information. Dig up your local community's history. You might go through old meeting minutes, yearbooks, or visit your local historical society. Again, harness technology to work for you! Find "that person" in your town or city who knows all the traditions and events. Work to discover what contributed to the school's culture in the community where you live or work today. Seek out stories related to genealogy, culture, heritage, traditions, and most importantly, people! Stories are what bring people together as a community, and then as a school community.

Ask the following questions:

1. **What is unique about your local community?**

    What makes your community special? Is there anything or anyone noteworthy about it in the past or the present? Is your community different from all others? How? Does your community serve a unique purpose for other communities? What makes it essential?

2. **What other communities are similar to your local community? What does your local community have in common with these other communities? How does your community/group help other communities?**

    Develop a visual representation for your answers to this question. If there is only one other community that you can compare/contrast to your own community, a Venn diagram will work fine. You could also use a table or chart to categorize this information, especially if you have other community groups to work with. Remember you are doing research not of just your own circle of influence, but the community it serves.

Strategic Tip #2:

Focus on your hometown community's school culture. This is an extremely important task if you really want to welcome and engage your students and families and what they value as you build your classroom's culture.

1. **How would you define and describe your community's culture? What do you and your students/families' value about the community?**

   If you want community members to value a group, they must choose to live out those values, even when away from the group. It is extremely difficult, if not impossible, to change a person's core values. Do not forget that as you work with people. When push comes to shove, you will see their "true colors" shining through. Are they invested in your group or are they just "going through the motions"?

2. **Ask questions, survey and interview others, and people watch. What are your findings?**

Observations will paint a picture of how people in your local community communicate and what they value as a culture. You will hear about heritage and history, triumphs and failures, emotions, and what is believed to be factual knowledge. Never underestimate the power of words and people watching…of all ages. It is amazing how little you may truly know about the community you are trying to connect with your group. Keep perspective in mind when you hear others speak. Remember, actions can speak louder than words.

3. **If changes were to happen, how would your community react? Why?**

Asking hypothetical questions can be tricky but doing so will help gauge how people might deal with change. It takes people different amounts of time to accept and embrace change. Just as starting a new job in a new place or meeting new people can be difficult, you need to think about what others would want to know before committing to any change. Once you have gathered that information, then you will need to think about the best way to have your group fit into a community. It is important that you recognize roadblocks at this point. If there are major red flags, do not keep moving forward until you address them.

Strategic Tip #3:

Finding your best fit keeps should come to mind when you work to reach any goal. Remember, by human design, everyone wants to fit in…to have a sense of belonging.

1. **What is the purpose of your own classroom in relation to connecting with the community?**

   Earlier in this book, I asked you to think about your purpose. I told you there would be a time when you would be called upon to write it down. Now is that time. Be sure to get input from others within your circle of influence. Make it a group effort. Be concise and use vocabulary that others will easily understand. Think about your organization's impact on the community.

2. **What does your classroom community promote? Does it emphasize human connections and relationships, including a valued sense of belonging and a purpose bigger than just one or two people?**

   If you want students to invest in your classroom, you need to know how to invest in what is important to them. Focus on how they promote relationships and how they communicate with each other. What will your classroom do to support continued connections with a sense of belonging? Make certain you never lose sight of what matters most…people!

Strategic Tip #4:

Revisit ethos, pathos, and logos. Human nature leads us to determine what matters most by using logic, checking in with our emotions, and following our gut feelings. Ask yourself the same questions that you believe they will ask themselves when making decisions about your classroom and learning.

1. **Why does this matter? What makes it valuable? Is there a sense of connection or commitment by an individual or group?**

   Why does any of this really matter? Simply put, this is the heart and soul of putting people first. You need to recognize the essential need of your students to feel connected if they are to commit their time and energy to a group. How will you offer that in your classroom community?

2. **Do your classroom goals equally appeal to the ethos, pathos, and logos of the hometown community and families?**

> If so, that is ideal. If not yet, it is okay, but the goal is to have all three of Aristotle's principles met by your organization. Your overall goal should be to have students who feel easily connected to your group, believing in its purpose, and wanting to serve it. Even if there is another community that has the same beliefs and/or the same goals, if your group can communicate ethos, pathos, and logos, it will be the chosen group to follow.

Strategic Tip #5:

Well, now that you have done your own super sleuthing of your local communities and families, you should begin to people watch and listen to others! This is quite fun and engaging. Encourage anyone within your circle of influence to do this activity. You will learn a plethora of information about what matters most to students and families!

1. Take plenty of notes, even audio recordings if possible, so you can review voice tone and word choice.

2. Oral histories are great to be able to reference as you study culture and community.

3. Be sure to engage in conversations with all generations in your community. Young and old!

4. Listen more, talk less! Be patient and let people collect their thoughts. What a terrific opportunity for your students to practice communication skills.

5. Consider inviting others to a light lunch or offering simple snacks to make your conversations more inviting.

Your Next Steps

After you determine who you are going to watch (and listen to), pay attention to the following:

- What seems to really matter to them?

- What about your goals and classroom culture matches what matters to them?

- What do they believe their purpose is in the community? What matters most to them? Do their individual values complement or contradict what you see and hear them telling you?

- Who appears to be leader of the students in your classroom? Is there someone who has power and someone else who has control? Do you know the difference? Watch and listen to people; you will find that not everyone in a power position by title actually has control in a group.

- Are you hoping to inform your students about your goal of creating a sense of belonging? Do you believe others will pay attention and listen? If so, what really piques their interest in conversations?

- Are you looking to build a case of persuasion to have them agree with you and/or disagree with another point of view or idea? Pay attention to how they behave when discussing assorted topics not related to your group. Group dynamics and behavior are great indicators of future behavior.

- Are you working to encourage students and families to engage/take part in your group or to meet a goal? If so, how do they initially react when you mention your goal?

All of these are uniquely different. By people watching, you will see group dynamics and behaviors appear within the community. Being aware of these behaviors ahead of time can allow you to be strategic in how you inform/persuade others.

In Conclusion

You see, human nature desires to make connections with others to fulfill a sense of belonging! Unfortunately, human relationships (ethos and pathos) are being challenged as we become more globally connected. People are unknowingly giving up true human interactions and connections.

Technology may appear to make human connections authentic, but only on a superficial level. No matter what, people still have an undeniable need for <u>all five senses</u> to be engaged to gain a sense of belonging. By harnessing social media, groups can continue conversations and connections that were built by face-to-face activities.

Local communities are where we build lasting relationships. By continuing to supply evidence that local community groups are not only practical, but vibrantly alive and essential, your educational institution and your classroom community can thrive. Choose to make it happen! Great communities make connections across all three points of Aristotle's work. How you make it a success is up to YOU!

8

Time for Your Own Circle of Influence

Pick <u>one</u> of the following as your circle of influence:

- Your classroom, your student families, and your colleagues
- Your school, faculty, staff, coaches, students, and families
- Or whoever you consider to be a target group to influence and encourage community growth.

While chapter seven was focused on the actual classroom community where you hope to have your students grow and flourish, this chapter is about your own circle of influence. The questions may look similar, but the focus is on <u>your group and your goals</u>. Be sure you follow that point of view!

1. **What is unique about your group/organization?**

   How is your group similar and different to groups/organizations in your local area vs. those in other geographic locations?

2. **How does your group currently fit in with your local community? What can your group provide to the community?**

   Is it a good fit? Do you bring something new, even a possible change to the community's culture? How will this engage and create a better version of those in the community?

3. **What makes your group unique and special to your clients? To your employees?**

   Make a detailed list of things that you feel are uniquely yours as an organization and what you can provide to the targeted community, as well as for your employees. Your employees will either be your biggest supporters or your worst critics. What makes them feel special?

4. **What does your group have in common with other organizations? For your clients? For your employees?**

    Make a list of those things you feel you have in common with other organizations and what you feel you both provide to a community. Are there differences or benefits that you both share? Is it possible you could build a partnership to grow even greater engagement in your community?

5. **Now that you have determined the cultural values of the local community, what are the cultural values of your own group?**

    This is an extremely important task if you really want to welcome and engage your community members and value their culture as you build your organization's culture. Ask questions, survey and interview others, people watch…all of these are observations will paint a picture of how people in your own group communicate and what they honestly value as a culture of workers. You will hear about heritage and family, triumphs and failures, emotions, and beliefs, and what matters most to them.

Never underestimate the power of words and people watching…of all ages. It is amazing how little you may really know about the people who are already invested in your group. Talk less and listen more! And, if change is to happen, you need to realize that it takes people different amounts of take to accept and embrace change. You need to think about those already invested members of your group and listen to their voice. Experience matters!

~~~~~~~~~

Super Sleuthing

Now that you have done both inside and outside super sleuthing, review the research you have done. Jot down and highlight the most important items you learned from your work. Creating a chart or visual representation is a terrific way to review all you have learned. Next, encourage people inside and outside of your organization to do the same work. Invite them to share whatever information they believe to be what most important to them and to the people they interact with in their own circle of influence. A sense of belonging is so important!

Aristotle's Art of Persuasion, One More Time

Take a few minutes to revisit ethos, pathos, and logos. Human nature leads us to determine what matters most when dealing with life. Is it a sense of importance to a given topic? Is it a sense of connection to an individual or group? What does any of this really matter? How are you making these connections happen within your organization? Ethos, pathos, logos. These three points are what make people, including students, feel like they can easily connect and be a part of your organizations, believe in its mission and vision as they work to meet the needs of your clients. It has employees who are committed to the success of the organization because they are a part of it. Even if there is another organization that has the same price point and the same mission, if you can communicate ethos, pathos, and logos, you will be the chosen organization by those in your community. You see, human nature desires to make connections with other that they can trust.

Human relationships (ethos and pathos) are what truly matter most in your classroom. As much as you may push the use of technology to be efficient, be sure you recognize it is limiting authentic human connections. If your students and families lose a sense of trust because they do not have genuine connections to you, your classroom will no longer thrive, it will merely survive. We can harness the role of social media to continue conversations that have been built on multiple platforms, but we innately still desire a smile and eye contact with those who we work with. Those foundational relationships are what local communities will always have and technology will always be in pursuit of creating. We must never lose sight of the value of one another. You need to make sure you continue to provide evidence that your classroom is not only viable in today's world, but it is vibrantly alive and essential for student learning. You need to be sure your students feel that same commitment to themselves as they provide to their friends. Great communities make connections across all three points of Aristotle's work. But how can we do this? Complete the *5W1H Self-Assessment* on the following page.

- Do this exercise independently first. Be sure to ask your other teacher colleagues within your school to also complete the self-assessment. Have them share what they see as important with you. This will lead to the creation of an overarching statement that your entire group has shared ownership of. You could do this by grade level team or content area. This builds a sense of teacher community within your own circle of influence.

- Do not ever forget your own people!

5W1H Self-Assessment

- **Who** do you want to inform, persuade, or engage in a conversation or activity? In this case, you might say students, parents, colleagues.
- **What** is your purpose as your plan to lead your classroom community?
- **Where, when,** and **how** does the mission you have for your classroom connect to your school's goal? Does it match your heart and soul goal(s) for your students?
- **Why** should students even care and want to engage with your classroom community?

Again, **when** you begin with your end goal in mind you are more likely to succeed. It makes everyone, including yourself more confident in what is being said and done with your organization, no matter **where** it is happening

A PLACE TO PONDER

9

Cornerstones of CCC

**CORNERSTONES OF CULTURE,
COMMUNITY AND COMMUNICATION**

Have a clear purpose.

Be personable and professional.

Study and value perceptions.

Focus on perspective.

Be proactive, not reactive!

Express positivity!

A cornerstone supports the foundation of a structure. It may be supporting a physical place, or it might be supporting an organization, business, school, community, or family. The five cornerstones shared in this chapter have tremendous value and importance. You must commit to each of them if you want to connect and engage with others. The value of culture, the importance of community, and the essential need for communication are built on these five cornerstones.

Choose to make all of them your own personal and professional cornerstones. Work diligently to build a sense of belonging in your community and organization.

- **Have a Clear Purpose**
- **Be Personable and Professional**
- **Study and Value Perceptions**
- **Focus on Perspective**
- **Be Proactive, Not Reactive**
- **Express Positivity**

Have A Clear Purpose

How do you create a clear purpose?

1. Review strategic tips #1 and #2, as well as the chapter entitled, "What is Your Ultimate Goal?"

2. Begin with your end goal in mind, but never lose sight of what is most important: building human relationships of value and substance.

Be Personable and Professional

Put people first and be a role model!

1. Make yourself approachable and use vocabulary that meets the audience and purpose you are communicating with.

2. Do not attempt to speak above or below people; speak their language. Be personable and professional!

3. Take the time to proofread, be formal in your communication.

4. Invest in others and others will invest in you. Put people first and find ways to make connections with them, beyond your projects or the bottom line.

Study and Value Perceptions

Just as we have our own perceptions of others and experiences that affected our lives, recognize so does every other person. Many times, people perceive things differently than we expect, plan, or intend. Based on each person's individual experiences and knowledge, they can easily have a different perception of the exact same topic. For example, schooling. We all may see value in learning, but our experiences with education and what we perceive as valuable can be drastically different from each another. Culture and community play a critical role in the perceptions people have on different topics.

Focus on Perspective

What do you want people to gain, maintain, or change based on their interaction with you or your group? Are you working to inform or persuade those people in your community? Are you hoping to lead others to be engaged supporters of your mission and activities?

1. Be clear and concise as you communicate in all ways (face-to-face, at a distance, online).
2. Be aware of the perspective you want others to have about you and your organization.
3. Work at using effective communication, minimizing interference.

Be Proactive, Not Reactive

As you work toward your goal of connecting and engaging others, be proactive in all you do. As much as possible, think ahead. Plan for the potholes and ways to avoid them. Plan for the worst, prepare for the best. Build relationships first and use a debit/credit system, where you are depositing as much as possible from the start of your relationships so you can build up a reserve. When difficulties arise, you will have already developed a sense of trust, which will help get you through the challenging times. Nothing in this world is perfect, but if you can work to be proactive rather than reactive, you will find it is much easier to solve problems and retain/regain relationships.

Express Positivity

Attitude is everything! You need to be clear when explaining your purpose, being personable as you share your vision with those in your community. And, if you know that you have some roadblocks and challenges ahead, do not express them with doubt or discontentment. Always focus on expressing positivity, even when things are not positive. This may prove difficult depending on your personality. But, remember, no one wants to engage in a community of naysayers and downers. You need to have a "can-do, will-do" attitude, no matter what! Be a positive leader!

RESOURCES

PERSONAL QUIZ

(There are no right or wrong answers!)

How do you prefer to communicate with others? Why?

How do you prefer <u>not to</u> communicate with others? Why?

What is your biggest challenge when communicating with others?

Think Tank Time #1

- What is your main purpose as a teacher? If asked, how would describe your classroom goals?

- Do you have a mission statement for your school? What about your own mission statement for your classroom community? Even if you do not, you should have a vision of what you hope to accomplish this year in tangible, actionable words.

- What words are integral and must be included in your teaching mission statement or vision statement? Take the time to not only list them but provide solid evidence for their value. Ask yourself why they are so important.

Think Tank Time #2

Everyone subconsciously asks these three questions
with each decision.

- What makes _____ important
  enough for my time and attention?

- Why should I care about _____?

- Will I support or not support _____ this
  purpose?

Think Tank Time #3

- How will you emphasize the importance of relationships in your plan to engage others?

- How will you effectively communicate your purpose with those in your community of learners?

- What do you feel will work best when persuading others to become engaged with your classroom community?

Think Tank Time #4

- What appeals to your students and their families?

- How can you affect them in a way that they want to be a part of your classroom community and mission?

- What are the goals, norms, values, believes, attitudes, traditions in your classroom?

- What is the center of your classroom community's culture?

Think Tank Time #5

Thinking about effective communication…

- How can you effectively communicate and share information with a larger audience in your local community to encourage participation in your school and classroom?

- How can you create opportunities for students to learn how to effectively communicate?

Think Tank Time #6

- What could be problems or interferences you may face when sharing your classroom mission, vision, and planned activities?

- How can you be most clear in communicating with your students and families?

- What about those who are not supporting your goals? How will you address them in a professional manner?

About the Author

Educator, coach, speaker, researcher, writer, consultant! During the past 23 years, Dr. Rebecca Speelman has collaborated with numerous community organizations, businesses, and educational institutions. In so doing, she has identified three key factors of personal success: culture, community, and communication. In this captivating and engaging book, she shows you how you can foster a true sense of belonging! You will learn how to find balance in your life, how you can ensure healthy human relationships, and how you can affect positive organizational leadership. Dr. Speelman will show you, in passionate detail, how you can make a change and how you can make a difference!

Please contact her at dr.rebecca.speelman@gmail.com if you are interested in booking a speaking engagement or a professional development workshop.

www.whybalancematters.com

Rebecca J. Speelman, LLC

ATCE: All Things Considered Education

Faith in Teaching

www.ingramcontent.com/pod-product-compliance
Lightning Source LLC
Chambersburg PA
CBHW022120280326
41933CB00007B/475